To: _Hamid_

D0888643

Game Changers extend the reach of those around them. In doing so they raise their own game. It's leadership for our times.

With best wishes

From: _[signature]_

This note book is 'work in progress'.

It's incomplete until you too have written your thoughts, ideas and **'notes to self'** in the spaces provided. There are three key questions woven into the fabric of this material...

1. How can you achieve greater fulfilment at work? Call this 'the inner game'.

2. How can you elevate the reach of those around you? Call this 'the outer game'.

3. How can you create 'leaders without title' at every level in your business? Call this 'the bigger game'.

You can't achieve 3 without 2. You can't achieve 2 without 1.

Published by Tools For Leading Change Ltd.
Copyright ©Sukhwant Bal, 2010.
ISBN 978-0-9553733-3-6

This 60 minute note book is for anyone in a Divisional, Functional or Corporate leadership role, in search of some elegantly simple and practical ideas. If you recognise yourself in any of this... then read-on...

- You're working 'full-on', doing the best you can with what you have, but you still feel you're fighting a losing battle. Just too much to do and not enough time. Your efforts just aren't being converted into breakthrough results. And the longer this goes on, the more drained you're becoming. **Work with one big idea from the 'inner game' section. Commit to it for one month.**

- Too much of your time is taken-up with sorting out 'politics'... rivalry between teams, point-scoring and lack of collaboration. Problems are being escalated to you, which should be resolved locally. At a time when people should be pulling together, they're pressing the 'self destruct' button. **Use the 'outer game' section for inspiration and partner with your senior colleagues to implement them.**

- Instinctively you know innovation in your business is required. Your customers, services and products are screaming out for it. Yet you can't seem to get any traction or momentum. Force of habits, change weariness and plain old cynicism are stifling your best intentions. **Deep-dive into the 'bigger game' section and shape a plan to develop leaders at every level in your business unit.**

'Game Changers' play by a different set of rules.

The game of business is hard enough, without the hardship of team conflict.

'Game Changing' top teams work to the motto – 'the competition is out there, not in here'.

'Game Changing' teams at the top live by **five** principles

1. We're in this together:
asking peers for support is a sign of strength, not weakness. Why wouldn't you engage some of the best brains in the business?

2. We team-up to tackle the big issues:
in doing so we uncover unexpected breakthroughs and innovations we could not have planned. In teaming-up, we also develop stronger working relationships.

3. We tap into each others' strengths:
we're in the results business and this demands we extend each others' reach. It's our insurance policy.

4. We get to the truth faster:
challenge each other in the pursuit of better decisions and stronger performance.

5. We have 'dual citizenship':
delivering results in our business area **AND** leading on the wider company agenda

These principles are not easy, a soft touch or require tree-hugging. The genius lies in freeing top teams... free to explore possibilities... free to collaborate. Just the conditions to innovate your way out of these difficult times.

The rules of the game have changed... for good.

Your reputation as a senior team is won and lost by what you do during the tough times. And the tough times are here.

When you've cut costs deeper than you dared... re-structured, re-designed and re-aligned... what next?

It's natural to go on the defensive and squeeze costs. Lean times forces you to focus on your core business. This simply buys you time. To re-group and take stock. But make no mistake, this places incredible stress on the business. You risk death by a thousand cuts.

You need more. An offensive strategy. One that helps you attract and retain customers over the long run. After all, this is what great brands are built on.

'Game Changers' pull together. It's a siege mentality. Us against the competition. We win or lose as a team.

Offensive strategy

New rules

In unprecedented times, work 'on' the business and 'in' the business

In difficult times the natural instincts of senior players is to work 'in' their business. It's tempting to work in your 'silo'. After all this is how you'll be measured and it's your neck on the line. Self preservation is a hard habit to kick.

Tough times demand more. Not more of the same. Operating in complex global markets is bigger than any one individual. It demands a new mindset.

Working **'on'** the business demands working beyond silos, Functions and Divisions. Exciting opportunities emerge by pooling the collective brains of senior players. After all, deep conversations generate ideas... ideas give birth to innovations... innovations create a competitive edge.

'Game Changing' senior teams work to an uncompromising set of values. The dominant one being... we're in this together. We all have individual **and** collective accountability. It's both. This takes courage. It raises the stakes.

The instincts of top teams...
a strong will to win

Ever noticed the psychological profile of people who make it to top teams?

For starters they have an extraordinary work ethic. Driven, utterly committed, type 'A' personalities. People who like to win... even when it's just for fun. Who eat and sleep work and make personal sacrifices for the business.

Let's not under-estimate their reasoning and organisational skills. Essential in managing complex projects on-the-run, in different geographies.

All of this demands self reliance. An unshakeable self belief, strong will and inner confidence to be in the driving seat. To be in control of work – not the other way around.

These qualities of driving results... honed over a life-time, opens the path to the top team. With a little luck along the way.

Yet all of these qualities, admirable though they are, are not conducive to great teamwork. And this is what top teams need to face up to. How do we need to play as one to create an agile organisation – able to manoeuvre with flair and speed – no matter what the market throws up.

This is winning on another scale. The triumph of 'we' over 'me'.

'Game Changers' convert opportunities into results

'Game Changers' are consumed by the need to create value for customers. To deliver this, they have no fear in working across boundaries. They see the organisational chart for what it is – dividing lines on paper only. So they actively manage the 'white spaces' on the organisational chart... by collaborating with other business units and functions.

'Game Changers' know they have to change their game first. They're all too aware that what got me here, won't get me there. So they make a choice... of seeing senior colleagues as partners, not rivals. And find every-day opportunities to co-create and simplify. They:

- Prototype new offerings and services. Run pilot projects, learn what works and what doesn't and scale up to create new markets.

- Re-design the customer experience... so internal teams regularly collaborate to fix problems at source.

- Win work, by exciting clients with a new kind of value proposition – combining the best of what the business has to offer.

'Game Changers' are not great visionaries. They're just better at teaming-up and in doing so, uncover hidden opportunities to do better business.

Their genius lies in creating their own luck.

The Leadership Gameplan

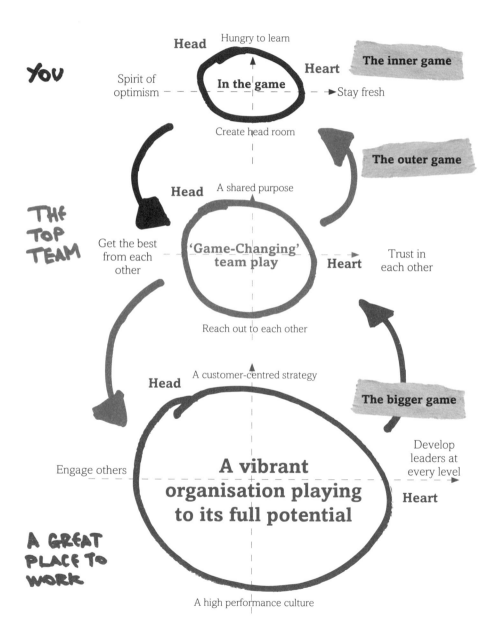

YOU

Head — Hungry to learn

Spirit of optimism — In the game — Stay fresh — Heart

The inner game

Create head room

THE TOP TEAM

Head — A shared purpose

The outer game

Get the best from each other — 'Game-Changing' team play — Trust in each other — Heart

Reach out to each other

A GREAT PLACE TO WORK

Head — A customer-centred strategy

The bigger game

Engage others — A vibrant organisation playing to its full potential — Develop leaders at every level — Heart

A high performance culture

Part 1: The Inner Game

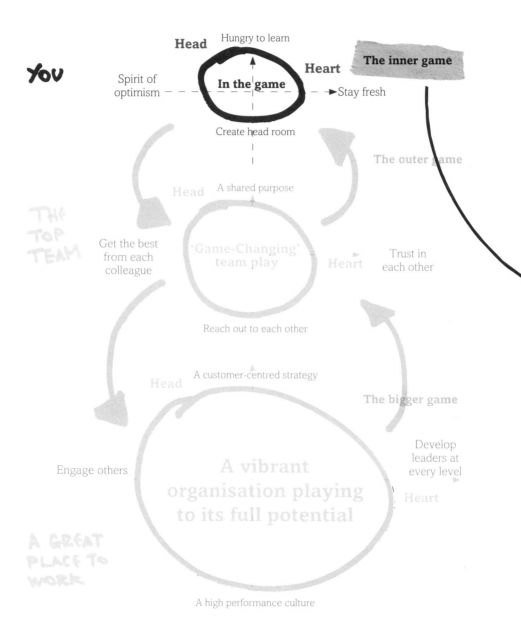

You

Head

Hungry to learn

The inner game

Spirit of optimism — — — In the game — — ➤ Stay fresh

Heart

Create head room

The outer game

A shared purpose

Head

Get the best from each colleague

'Game-Changing' team play

Heart

Trust in each other

THE TOP TEAM

Reach out to each other

A customer-centred strategy

Head

The bigger game

Engage others

A vibrant organisation playing to its full potential

Develop leaders at every level

Heart

A GREAT PLACE TO WORK

A high performance culture

You owe it to yourself to play your best game.
You don't have to look far. The answer lies within.

As a senior player it's too easy to run on empty. There will always be too much to do and not enough time. It's a trap.

It's too easy for deadlines and pressures to leave you feeling jaded, exhausted and frustrated. It's hard to lead yourself, let alone others when you feel battle scarred.

So you have an obligation to look after yourself.
To be centred and self aware.

Find your spark...
a cause you believe in

It's a given - being part of a top team comes with pressures.

It's the nature of the game. Problems, priorities, deadlines... can weigh you down. Extinguish your fire. Leave you feeling as though you're running on empty.

Learn to manage the pressures or 'they' will manage you.

The minutia and your day-to-day headaches need to be put in perspective. But you can only do this if you have a 'juicy idea'. For some it's their 'purpose'. For others it's their 'rallying call'... BHAG (Big Hairy Audacious Goal)... dream... inspiration... call it what you will - it makes coming into work worthwhile.

Listen to your customers. Look at the market trends. Spend time 'on the shop floor'. Get out there and find your spark. Uncover innovations to set your business apart. Find a cause you can be energised and excited by. If you don't know what's important, you'll be consumed with the 'urgent' and with it the frustration of chasing your tail.

A spirit of optimism - hope over defeatism

The buck stops with you.

It comes with the job. The stuff others find too difficult to handle will get escalated to you. And this constant diet of tough calls, problems and conflict can wear you out emotionally.

The danger signs come when you begin to question yourself - your capabilities, your judgement and your self worth. The demands are high enough, without piling even more pressure on yourself. By all means take stock and learn from your mistakes. But don't let this tip-over into destructive self talk. This will just eat away your confidence... bit by bit. And this is why self-talk is so poisonous. It works by stealth.

Optimism is not a soft option. It's heavy-duty armouring. And it works when you turn off the negative mood music. Your challenge is to kill pessimism and to do that you need to regulate your inner dialogue. Most of our anxieties are irrational and will never materialise. Yet feeding these fears gives them a life they don't deserve.

Mellow yellow - be resilient

Mental toughness sees us through adversity. It's the ability to tough it out and persevere in the face of hardships and intense high profile situations.

But how do you stay grounded, balanced and level-headed in the small, everyday trials of business?

Choose your battles wisely. Don't let every problem wear you down. It's called perspective. Learn to distinguish the minor blip from the major blow-out.
Talk things through with trusted colleagues. There's a danger to 'bottling things up'.
You can become trapped – with destructive thought patterns feeding off each other.
So much of our thinking happens on 'automatic pilot' we're unaware of it.
Precisely the reason why negative thinking can eat away at your self confidence and sense of perspective.

Next, look for solutions not someone to blame. When the heat is on, don't get consumed by flames of anger. It creates an adverse reaction – defensive behaviour. People cover things up, deflect the blame and you get selective information.
Your chances of sorting out the problem have just diminished.

Give yourself the best chance of clear thinking. Take lunch away from your desk. Go for a walk. Do some form of physical activity. When you're running on empty... these simple steps boost your energy.

An attitude of gratitude - the best stress buster

You have a duty of care - for the wellbeing of your organisation and the people in it. But who will care about you?

When the days are long and the demands keep coming, the gloss of the role can soon wear off. Stress seeps in and it has a habit of distorting reality. You can find yourself losing your temper over trivial things. It's a dangerous pattern, especially if you're at the top. Every slip-up gets noticed, magnified and is out in the open.

Your protection is elegantly simple. Self motivation. Reconnect with the original reason you chose this path. You're fulfilling an ambition to build a strong team, to deliver great services and to make a mark. You're pursuing a worthy prize. And the prize no one can deny is the sense of personal satisfaction – when you see team members stepping up and winning. Every personal challenge you encounter is meant to be. This is personal development of the highest order. You will make mistakes... a sure sign you're working at the limits and pushing the boundaries.

Learn to have fun today. Enjoy now. It's a mistake to measure your success and self worth on goals you may achieve sometime in the future. It's a mirage. So don't build your happiness on tomorrow.

Hungry to learn – move with the times

The rate of change 'out there' is phenomenal.

For this reason alone, your rate of learning needs to keep pace with it.
When the rules of the game are being continuously re-written, this forces your hand.
Keep re-inventing yourself or risk being left behind.

When the heat is on, our instincts are to do more. We rush to apply the rules and tactics which have worked for us in the past. The trap is set. Past success is no guarantee of future success. Learning agility is a senior players' life-line. Cut this and you risk being left adrift. Deemed as having had your day, living on past glory and stuck in your ways.

The message is simple. Stay curious. Be open to new ideas and be willing to experiment. We re-invent ourselves by experiencing a different diet and seeing things through a different lens. Exposure to different stimuli, cultures, teams and challenges creates your awakening. So take the plunge.

Be still.

Create head room ←

Reflect on what's working and what isn't.

Re-group and Re-focus.

Create head-room - time to think, reflect and ponder

When you're full-on, all of the time, the world can pass you by in a blur.

You fly from one deadline to another, your schedule crammed and your time squeezed – and before you know it, it's quarter-end, mid-year and 12 months have flown by.

If everything is important – then nothing is important. So develop the skill of focus. Very deliberately create islands in your diary. Time when you can cut yourself off from the background noise. The distractions, emails, calls and requests for information.

Be still. Re-group and re-focus. Reflect on what's working and what isn't. Scan the horizon and see the potential warning signs. Surround yourself with colleagues who will tell it to you like it is.

Reflect and re-calibrate. This is your chance to simplify your life. To identify the big ticket items you need to deliver and the 'next wave' you need to be ready for.

In a nutshell

To play your best game - every day - take care of your psychological wellbeing. In doing so, you can give more of your true self. It's the core of being an authentic leader.

When you're tired your 3lb 'skull computer' is prone to 'virus attack'. So you read into things. Become hyper-critical. Say things you wish you could retract. Make one too many poor judgement calls.

Press the pause button. Find silence in the eye of the storm.

Stand back from the heat and to take a cooler, detached perspective.
Stay focused on where you want to get. Keep up-dating your plans.
Go public on them. Nothing maintains energy and motivation like progress.
Those around you will feed-off your will-to-win and enthusiasm.

Before you can lift others' spirits, you have to replenish yours.

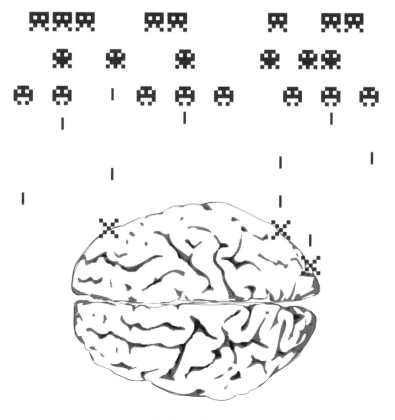

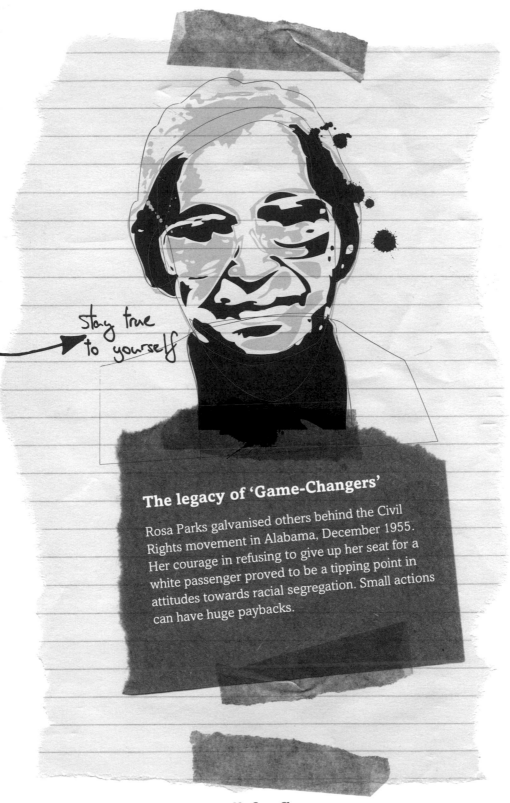

Stay true to yourself

The legacy of 'Game-Changers'

Rosa Parks galvanised others behind the Civil Rights movement in Alabama, December 1955. Her courage in refusing to give up her seat for a white passenger proved to be a tipping point in attitudes towards racial segregation. Small actions can have huge paybacks.

Part 2: The Outer Game

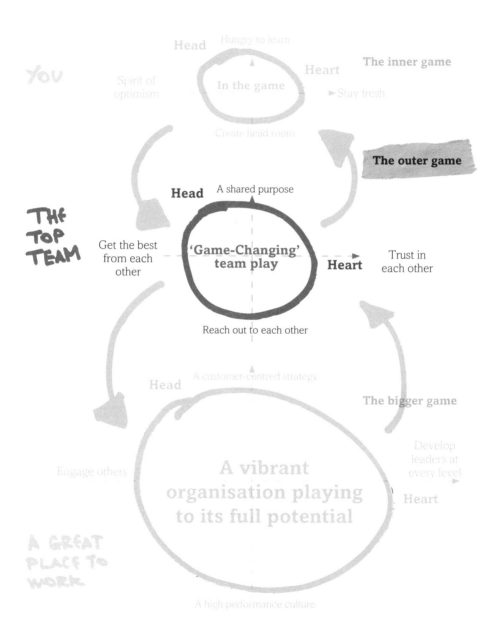

You

Head — Hungry to learn

The inner game

Spirit of optimism

In the game

Heart — ▶ Stay fresh

Create head room

The outer game

THE TOP TEAM

Head — A shared purpose

Get the best from each other

'Game-Changing' team play

Trust in each other

Heart

Reach out to each other

A customer-centred strategy

Head

The bigger game

A vibrant organisation playing to its full potential

Engage others

Develop leaders at every level ▶

Heart

A GREAT PLACE TO WORK

A high performance culture

When the top team come together, what do you see?

Competitors or collaborators?

'Game changing' top teams create space to discuss hopes, concerns, threats and fears. The things everyone thinks but no one articulates.

This simple act of 'speaking up' with courage, especially during tough times, is often the springboard to take top team performance to another level.

Are you a...
Collaborator
or
Competitor?

Painting by numbers

Look around you.

The make-up of most senior teams is driven by one thing – *organisational structure*. Individuals turn up wearing their Functional or Business Unit hats.

The problems start when these hats never come off. And team members 'play in their box'. Individuals only contribute when it's relevant to their business or function. This may be good meeting etiquette. But hardly the stuff of passionate debate.

A group coming together to report on results and numbers does not make for a team. In fact it can have the feel of rivals. Who reveal little, score a few points when the opportunity arises and go back to what they really care about – leading their own teams.

You can feed this monster or you can slay it.

Hand-on-heart: what are you prepared to give to this team?

Let's get to the heart of the matter.

You may have 'team' in your title – *'senior management team'* – but this does not mean you behave as one. A **team** and a **group** are poles apart in the spirit, energy and relationships. One is 'agenda' driven and the other is 'purpose' driven.

Agenda driven groups 'plug-in' and 'plug out'. Individuals scan down the agenda, see when they're 'on' and dutifully present. But they 'pull the plug out' when the discussion moves 'off-my-patch'. So you see colleagues checking their texts and emails... preparing for their next meeting... there in body but not in mind. These ritualistic meetings are tiring for everyone. They take lot of time and effort to prepare but with little return.

Corporate governance does not have to be this dull.

Purpose driven teams face-up to reality. We are in this together. The competition is 'out there' and not 'in here'. Given business is so complex, so fast changing, so unpredictable - we have to pull together. And this simple truth creates the conditions for collaboration.

'Game Changers' ask for support and willingly reach out to peers.

A shared purpose: how we'll make this business great.

When you ask employees what the senior team can improve, 'direction' comes high on their list. This often catches senior teams by surprise... 'what do you think we've been communicating these past months'?

Yet it's understandable. If a strategy is not compelling, it's instantly forgettable. The art lies in amplifying it. Bring real world examples to it, so employees can truly connect with it. Stories stick where bland facts don't.

Add to this the complexity of shaping strategy during a recession. In striving to survive and manage the pressures on costs, headcount and re-structuring – strategy is too easily 'put on hold'. Today dominates. Tomorrow can wait.

Yet employees will 'take the pain' now, if they can see how they'll benefit in the future. And this is the ace card strategy holds. It gives meaning and context. Without it, people are working in the dark. They lose sight of why they're pushing themselves and work becomes a drudge.

As a business what will we be famous for? In a crowded market place this becomes a 'must-answer' question. Working this through will bring you closer together as a senior team. It requires you to listen, to question and to put yourself in each others' shoes. These behaviours foster openness - a precursor to trust.

Trust in each other:
but you have to earn it first

Trust is fragile.

Yet any team, especially a senior team, will find it hard to function without it. Trust has currency. It opens the way for honest conversations. What is a top team if it is not capable of this? Effective decision making needs all colleagues to have a voice and express what they really think.

Settle for 'healthy tension'. Trust based teams hold each other to real scrutiny and challenge. They strive to get the best from each other. And that's the basis of trust based relationships. There is an explicit understanding team members challenge, question and debate in the spirit of raising the team's performance. It's all in the intent. It's not about positioning, politics or power.

How to earn trust? It starts with your level of self disclosure and honesty with the team. It begins with not 'sugar coating' difficult news. Pin pointing what went wrong and accepting your responsibilities. It's putting team ahead of 'ego'. Your integrity and trust is also enhanced when you don't take advantage of others' failures. Point scoring, sarcasm and inappropriate humour, amounts to putting your 'trust account' in the red.

Learn how to get the best from colleagues

The curse of any team is having 'insiders' and 'outsiders'.

Those who dominate air-time and those who rarely contribute. This simply creates dysfunctional team work. Just think of the intellectual horse power being wasted.

Strong values are critical for the well-being of any team. Like respect, showing appreciation, listening and having fun. Strong, confident, independent players have to appreciate they can learn from their peers. As a senior player your growth comes from being 'inclusive'. Recognise the strengths in the colleagues around you and harness these for the benefit of the team.

Fact is every team member has signature strengths – beyond their Functional or technical capabilities. Those colleagues who have a knack of simplifying the complex and in doing so help the team get 'unstuck'. Those creative types who turn a problem on its head and spot the opportunities, somehow missed by everyone else. The analytical colleagues who get under-the-skin of customer data and pin point critical connections. You get the picture. Find the opportunities to help peers shine. This simple act elevates your credentials as a principled leader.

The real work begins outside of formal meetings. Make time for a coffee. Learn about peers as individuals first and senior players second.

Reach out to each other: this sets the standard for teams.

'Silo' working survives on the back of one trump card – accountability.

It's my neck on the line. Senior players reckon 'I need to get my own back yard in order if I'm to have credibility with my peers'. Yet over-playing this card kills collaboration. Team work dies. In it's place - survival of the fittest.

Collaboration feeds innovation and wealth creation. When colleagues grasp their inter-dependence and see we're all in the same boat, facing the same challenges and headaches - it's easier to reach out to each other.

Your customers suffer when the 'hand over' points between teams are mismanaged. When Production complain Manufacturing have given them poor quality material. When Sales complain R&D is developing the wrong product, when Logistics complain Sales are agreeing unrealistic timescales for delivery.

Before these situations arise... reach out. Have the difficult conversations. Clear the air. Resolve the 'friction points'. When senior players 'play ball', others join-in. This frees your time to work on the exciting stuff.

Functional hat and senior team hat: (both) hats are essential

Dual 'corporate citizenship' comes with the job.

You have to work **'in'** the business and **'on'** the business. Two very different skill sets.

Working 'in' the business for most players is their comfort-zone. These are the projects and priorities that need to be implemented – now – in your business unit or function.

Your days will be consumed by operational meetings, leaving room for little else.

Is it any wonder that senior players find working 'on' the business less appealing? For starters they're exhausted by the 'now'. Can't the future take care of itself? In turbulent times can a senior team really define a strategy that's worth the paper it's written on? Isn't it out of date, before the printer ink is even dry?

Yet, working 'on' the business is critical. This is your articulation of how we as a business will stand-out from the competition. It clarifies your uniqueness, your strengths and your intent. Call it purpose... strategy... a 'game plan'... either way it matters.

Articulating this gets you all on the same page as a leadership team. Don't under-estimate the strength of this. It 'pulls' you together.

In a nutshell

'Game Changing' top teams know that by pulling together they'll achieve more. Internal competition has its place – but not in top teams.

Collaboration is not the easy option. Far from it. Senior players are highly independent and enjoy autonomy. Yet by curbing this urge, they show powerful leadership to the rest of the organisation. One team, role modelling the company's values, working for the good of the 'whole'... endorses your credibility as a team, more clearly than anything else. Actions speak louder than words.

In a networked world, senior teams need to take on the role of 'partners' not rivals. Efficiencies and innovations emerge when business units and functions team-up, to learn from each other.

The legacy of 'Game-Changers'

Roger Bannister broke the 4 minute mile in Oxford, May 1954. With the support of two fellow runners of Brasher and Chataway, he laid to rest the myth it was impossible to run the sub 4 minute mile. Just 46 days later John Landy on June 21st set a new world record. From that date the mile world record has been broken 17 times.

Bannister's record confirms we can all achieve more by joining forces with others. And extend each others' reach. Truth is, new records require game-changing thinking.

Part 3: The Bigger Game

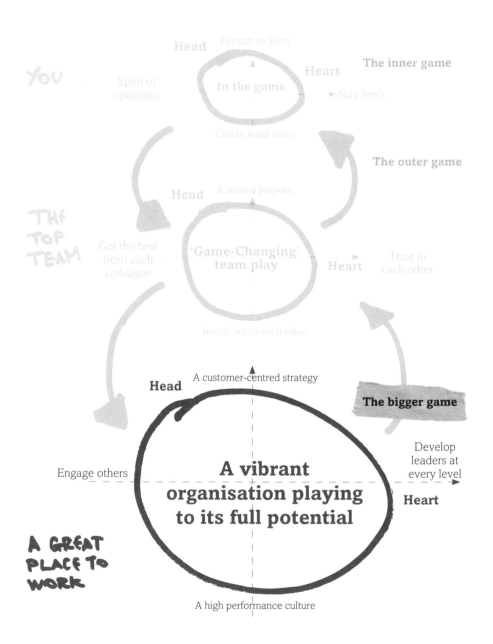

YOU

Head · Hungry to learn · Heart

The inner game

Spirit of optimism · In the game · ►Stay fresh

Create head room

The outer game

Head · A shared purpose

THE TOP TEAM

Get the best from each colleague · 'Game-Changing' team play · Heart · Trust in each other

Reach out to each other

Head

A customer-centred strategy

The bigger game

Engage others

A vibrant organisation playing to its full potential

Develop leaders at every level

Heart

A GREAT PLACE TO WORK

A high performance culture

How can 'the few' engage 'the many'?

Top teams can unwittingly stifle the energy and innovation latent in their organisation.

To unleash it, treat employees as investors...
who have a choice. They can put more of themselves into work, or do 'just enough'. It comes down to discretionary goodwill.

Remember, you can't pay for it, you can only inspire it.

'Game Changing' top teams work hard to strengthen leadership at every level of their organisation.

Game changers can score 'own goals'

Senior teams have position power.

There is no denying this. So your words, actions and behaviour matter – big time.

Here's how it works. People come into work to do a good job. No one deliberately intends to sabotage the business. But toxic and inappropriate working habits can set in. It's subtle. But the effects can be cumulative and devastating.

Want some examples?

The Sales Director who in front of their team bad-mouths the Operations Director – in jest or with sarcasm – but the tone is set. This then gets played-out by Sales people picking holes with what Ops does... it slowly eats away at trust, openness and team work between these two functions. Poisonous words create toxic reactions.

It doesn't stop there.

When senior players work in 'silos', fail to manage the 'white spaces' on the organisational chart, become defensive when colleagues feel they're not getting full collaboration... this has a nasty habit of being played out further down the organisational chart.

Rather than 'one company' working to one shared goal, you get fiefdoms and tribal warfare.

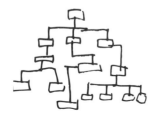

Develop leaders at every level

Leadership is a mindset.

It's not related to position or job title. It's an attitude of walking towards challenges, taking them on and winning. Leaders care enough to challenge poor service, processes and ways of working. They won't walk-by.

In 'backs to the wall' situations, organisations need leaders to step up. The top team can only see so much and do so much. It's the people closer to the front-line and closer to customers who are best positioned to make the right choices.

'Game Changing' top teams take their message out into the business. Through eye-ball contact with employees, they encourage people to show courage and to step up. They create the conditions for employees to bring all of themselves to work – their **hands**, their **heart** and their **head**. They don't just demand this. They encourage it. Through regular workshops and forums they unleash people to act in the best interest of the business. These forums address real issues, in real time, with the right colleagues in the room.

Let's be clear. These are NOT 'power-point' driven, one-way channels of communication.

Leadership is a mindset. It's not related to position or job title.

Top teams take their message out into the business.

Engage employees... do they 'turn-up' or are they 'turned-on' by work?

Knowledge workers won't accept 'command-and-control' management. They know their worth, have opinions and are willing to articulate them.

What's more they don't respect title or status. They're not deferential. They can choose to give their discretionary goodwill – or withhold it. Withholding goodwill often amounts to not returning phone calls and emails promptly... providing information but failing to explore the context. The technical aspects of the job get done. But service leaves a lot to be desired.

'Game Changing' top teams know engagement is a precursor to high performance. For this reason they treat employees as 'internal investors'. Taking every opportunity to communicate future direction, strategy and how we'll outsmart the competition. Even if this is being formulated they 'go public'. After all, every business needs 'early adopters'.

Employees engage with a business they trust in. They believe it has a place in the world, adds value to customers and the communities they're apart of. The company's 'reason for being' goes beyond shareholder return. It has a set of values, culture and ethos they want to be apart of. They experience it. And the actions and behaviours of the top team, endorses this belief.

The No.1 job for every employee is to deliver for their customers

How best can senior teams stir the organisation into purposeful action?

It's easy to create busyness. The challenge is to direct maximum attention to those activities which will return maximum payback. And all roads lead to customers.

Challenge anything which distracts employees from serving customers – for today or for tomorrow. It's simple economics. In a 'supply and demand' world, your products and services need to be continually keeping pace with changing customer demands.

The reality is, employees are closer to customers than senior players. They know at first hand the customer complaints and gripes. They know what adds value and what doesn't.

It helps if senior teams 'get back to the shop floor'. Make this a routine of how you do business. Get out-there. Put yourself in your employees' shoes and see, hear and feel their highs and lows. This will tell you more than any reports and statistics on your customers' experience.

Employees need to feel pride in their organisation. If employees don't care, you can bet your customers will experience it. 'Game-Changing' teams free their front-line employees to get it right for the customer – absolutely. But their ambition goes much further. They create frequent forums for employees to become 'game changers' too. Chances for them to pitch their ideas to the top team and receive 'go', 'no-go' decisions. This creates a constant feedback cycle between front-line colleagues and upper management. It speaks volumes. One organisation, dedicated to improving the customer experience.

Improve the customer experience!

Create a performance culture: where people manage their own performance - first.

Senior teams are in the results business.

They're very aware of what figures they need to hit: profit, revenue, market share, growth... and there is no shortage of measures and metrics to tell them how they're doing. This clear-cut definition of success can create some unforeseen consequences.

In chasing the 'what', the 'how' is not given proper attention. Goals merely define the finishing line. But how the race will be run and paced is of equal importance. Especially if you're in it for the long-run. It's too easy to peak early. To burn yourself and your team out, in hitting this quarter's results or this year's targets.

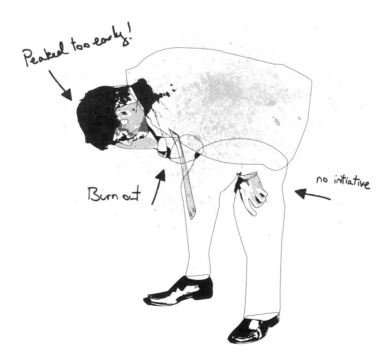

....

Be wary of imposing 'top-down' initiatives. It dulls initiative taking, creativity and ownership. You create 'learned behaviour'. Employees act and respond as '<u>order takers</u>'. They escalate problems back to you. Seek your approval. Want you to make the decisions.

What if you were to see employees as 'investors' – who turn up to work not just for financial rewards – but psychological returns? Seeking fulfilment, satisfaction and personal growth. This is the guiding principle behind creating a performance culture. If you coach colleagues to work for themselves first and the company second, you create the mindset of 'owner-managers'. People who give more and care more. Who enjoy work, rather than endure it.

Seeking fulfilment ⟶

satisfaction ⟶

personal growth ⟶

In a nutshell

Vibrant organisations have a beating heart.

Irrespective of good times or bad - people deliver for the customer.

This is the power of organisational culture. People expect more from themselves than anyone else. They have the 'skill' and 'will' to step-up. It's called leading without title. When enough people care and choose to manage their own performance - first... your customers benefit. You can't demand people enjoy work, or feel motivated by work - but you can create the right conditions.

This is what 'Game Changing' top teams understand. Like it or not, your behaviour, visibility and leadership have a massive gravitational pull on the rest of the organisation. To create a great place to work, free people to be 'game changers'. To do great work and know it'll be appreciated.

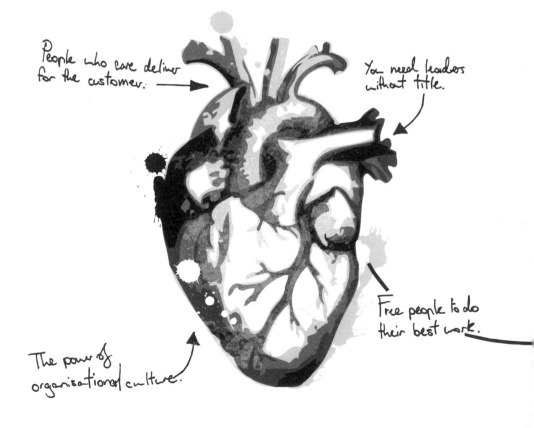

People who care deliver for the customer.

You need leaders without title.

Free people to do their best work.

The power of organisational culture.

The legacy of 'Game-Changers'

In the 1500s Florence (Tuscany) experienced a renaissance, with an explosion of breath-taking art, innovations and writing. The likes of Leonardo da Vinci, Michelangelo and Raphael, leaving their mark on the world. Historians credit this amazing period to the concentration of 'creative minds', in such a small area. Each bringing the genius best out of each other.

When (you) play your best game, incredible things happen!

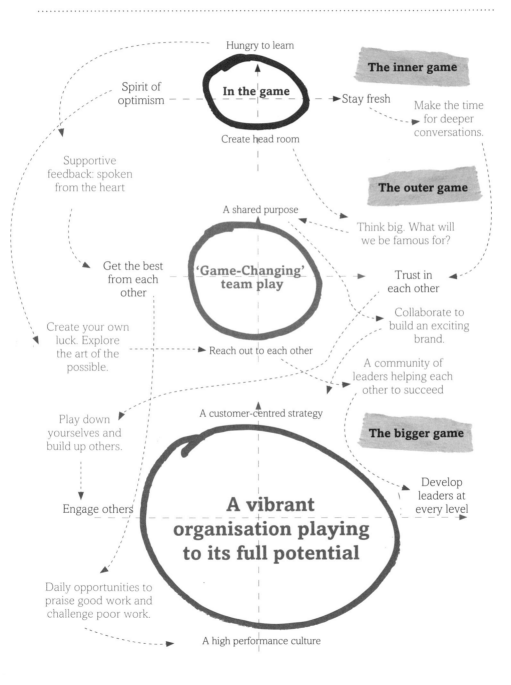

Hungry to learn

The inner game

Spirit of optimism — — — **In the game** — — ►Stay fresh

Make the time for deeper conversations.

Create head room

Supportive feedback: spoken from the heart

The outer game

A shared purpose

Think big. What will we be famous for?

Get the best from each other

'Game-Changing' team play

Trust in each other

Collaborate to build an exciting brand.

Create your own luck. Explore the art of the possible.

Reach out to each other

A community of leaders helping each other to succeed

A customer-centred strategy

The bigger game

Play down yourselves and build up others.

Develop leaders at every level

Engage others

A vibrant organisation playing to its full potential

Daily opportunities to praise good work and challenge poor work.

A high performance culture

Closing thoughts: why be a 'Game Changer'?

You've reached the end of this note book... And possibly one question has gone unanswered... What's in it for you? Why be a 'Game Changer'?

Shape your own future.
Past success is no guarantee of future success. Right now the rules of the game are being re-written... the leadership agenda is shifting... big time. Be a part of this renaissance towards a stronger values based, ethical and customer-centred leadership.

Punch above your weight.
Role model leadership through your everyday actions. 'Game Changers' give freely... their support, encouragement and wisdom. Be a team player who elevates others' game. Generosity has a habit of being repaid.

Stay hungry, keep learning.

The rule of thumb is 'the more demanding the role, the faster you have to adapt'. Be self aware, play to your strengths and recognise the warning signs that trigger negative reactions. Be bold and see big challenges as opportunities for personal growth.

Collaborate to innovate.

It's no longer about your individual brilliance. It's now about how quickly you can generate value through networks, teams, communities and alliances. Go on, reach out.

Pursue your cause.

You boost your energy, passion and commitment when you truly believe in what you're doing. When work has meaning and you chase worthwhile goals, the setbacks and problems along the way get put into perspective. At every opportunity connect others behind your cause. Win backers... you can't do without them.

Our Core Leadership Programme

Phase 1: Play your best game. A 2 day workshop supported with 360 degree feedback, intensive coaching and the formulation of a personal development plan. This workshop rejuvenates leaders. The outcome is a 'game plan' to play to their strengths, feel energised and excited by their big ticket challenges. The focus is clear. How do you personally need to raise your game and 'punch above your weight'?

Follow up activities

Phase 2: 'Game Changing' team work. A 2 day workshop to begin building team cohesion, trust and a shared purpose. Through skilful facilitation we guide an intact team through the 'unspoken truths'... are we working to a powerful shared agenda, are we getting the best from each other and are we taking this business to new heights?

Follow up activities

Phase 3: A vibrant organisation: playing to its full potential. A 2 day workshop on how to build leadership capability at every level and create a great place to work. After all, leadership is a 'contact sport'. The outcome from this workshop will be a 12 month 'engagement' plan. The means to harness the talent and energy in the business towards our strategy.

Follow up activities.

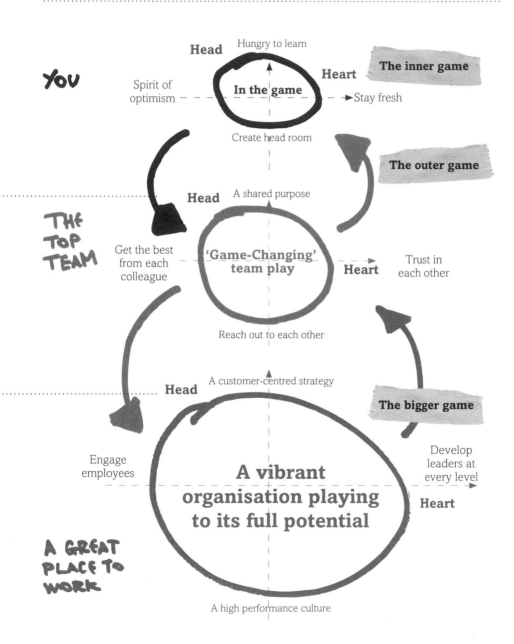

YOU

Head — Hungry to learn — Heart

In the game

Spirit of optimism — Stay fresh

Create head room

The inner game

The outer game

THE TOP TEAM

Head — A shared purpose

'Game-Changing' team play

Get the best from each colleague — Heart — Trust in each other

Reach out to each other

The bigger game

A customer-centred strategy

Head

Engage employees

A vibrant organisation playing to its full potential

Develop leaders at every level

Heart

A GREAT PLACE TO WORK

A high performance culture

Our ethos in helping you, our clients succeed

Over the last 20 years we've been fortunate to work with some great clients. Our recent projects have taken us to: Copenhagen, Amsterdam, Dubai, Hong Kong, Mumbai, San Francisco, Milan and Frankfurt. We are a UK based team, willing to be where our clients need us. We hold dear six core values.

Psychologists with pragmatism.

We are a team of Corporate Psychologists. It's our passion and our vocation. It's the underpinning to our leadership, coaching and team development work. But we never preach or give you text book answers. We use applied psychology to get to the real root causes... so you create an organisation fit to compete, win and achieve impressive results.

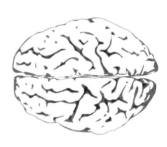

Grounded in your business.

We commit to understanding your business, goals and priorities. In doing so, we'll invest our own time, without charge to you. We'll tailor workshop language and content to reflect your business culture.

The tools to ensure you become self reliant.

We have built our reputation on developing tools, tips and templates to ensure real learning and actions continue, long after the Consultants have left. We will help you to fly solo.

It's all about the relationship
It's never about the fees.

Our raison d'être is adding value and making a difference to the success of your business. Almost exclusively our business comes through existing relationships, who pass our name on to their contacts. We know our fees are highly competitive. We won't charge you for travel time and we also give a lot back with pro bono coaching. It's our service commitment to you.

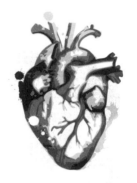

Lasting results: we're not fans of 'one-off' workshops.

A workshop is a starting point, not an end-point. So we work with you to build in 'check-points', evaluate progress and to connect workshop outcomes with other internal initiatives... performance, talent and succession plans.

A spirit of partnership.

We believe strong relationships are grounded in honest conversations and mutual respect. We're serious about our work – but we don't take ourselves too seriously.

From the author

It's evident from our consulting work, how this global recession has rocked individuals and organisations.
With greater uncertainty and insecurity, there is a natural urge to scan for danger... to be cautious, to tread with care, to be on the defensive.

But what do you do, when you've done all the obvious things to get your business back on track? How do you free people to act with courage and confidence?

Let's not forget senior teams themselves are not immune to these strong human emotions... of doubt and anxiety. And over a sustained period, results in fatigue, burnout and poor results.

It doesn't have to be this way. 'Game Changers' play to a different model, founded on strong values of teamwork and collaborative behaviour. We live in a networked world. Relationships and connections count. And 'Game Changers' recognise they can't ignore these fundamentals.

The aim of this note book and Game Changers Toolkit is to offer ideas and insights to help you elevate your game, at a time when we need strong leadership from senior teams – like never before.

I'd welcome any feedback and your stories of implementing 'game changing' practices.

With best wishes

Sukhwant

Sukhwant

+44 (0)7768 507248

Our other publications and products.

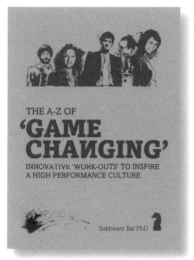

The A-Z Innovation Toolkit. 52 practical 'work-outs' for creating a high performance culture.

The Power To Inspire Handbook:
Pre-reading for our 100 Watt Coaching programme. Along with a set of Values Cards, Support Cards and Feedback Cards.

Coaching For Change Handbook: Pre-reading for our 'Coaching For Change' workshop. Supported by: The Leader as Coach Questionnaire and 'Knowing-Doing' Gap Analysis.

Our other publications and products.

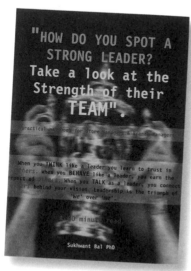

How Do You Spot A Strong Leader Handbook? Pre-reading for our workshop on high potentials transitioning to new roles. Insights into what to 'stop' doing to be effective in a new role.

Careers, Customers and Cash Handbook: A director's guide to mentoring and building a great business: pre-reading for our Mentoring workshops. A unique framework for identifying how to add value at different job levels. How 'what got you here, won't get you there'.